SCHIRMER'S LIBRARY
OF MUSICAL CLASSICS

Vol. 1399

EDVARD GRIEG

Concerto

For Piano

Opus 16

With the Orchestral Accompaniment
Arranged for a Second Piano

Edited, Revised, Fingered, Pedalled and with Explanatory

Remarks by

PERCY GRAINGER

G. SCHIRMER, Inc.

DISTRIBUTED BY

7777 W. BLUEMOUND RD. P.O. BOX 13819 MILWAUKEE, WI 53213

FOREWORD

Edvard Grieg, who was born at Bergen, Norway, in 1843, composed his piano concerto in 1868, at the age of twenty-five, while spending the summer vacation in the Danish village of Sölleröd, Zealand, one year after his marriage with Nina Hagerup, his cousin.

In Mr. Henry T. Finck's authoritative and inspiring book "Grieg and His Music" (which should be consulted by all lovers of Grieg's music and personality, since it was the one of all the Grieg biographies the most highly prized by Grieg himself) we read the following regarding the concerto:

It is a model in the way in which it avoids both of the common defects of being either a symphony with pianoforte accompaniment or a showpiece for the soloist with orchestral accompaniment. It is, above all things, good music—delightful music, provided it is played by one who understands its deep poetic spirit.... The Grieg concerto is now a classic, an inevitable number in the repertory of all the great pianists.... The first movement is replete with beautiful, haunting melody, and nothing could be more lovely than the orchestral introduction to the slow movement—one of the saddest preludes ever written—a prelude illustrating Grieg's gift of creating an emotional atmosphere with the simplest means—a gift which, as Rudolf M. Breithaupt has remarked, would be useful to many a contemporary composer. Grieg knew full well that he had given to the world an immortal work, and he continued to improve it to the end.

Earlier in Mr. Finck's book we read the following interesting episode in connection with Liszt's characteristically far-seeing and warm-hearted reception of the Grieg concerto:

Grieg's second meeting with Liszt.... was no less interesting than the first. It is thus described by him:

"I had fortunately just received the manuscript of my pianoforte concerto from Leipzig, and took it with me.... Winding and I were very anxious to see if he would really play my concerto at sight. I, for my part, considered it impossible; not so Liszt. "Will you play?" he asked, and I made haste to reply: "No, I cannot" (you know I never practised it). Then Liszt took the manuscript, went to the piano, and said to the guests, with his characteristic smile: "Very well, then, I will show you that I also cannot." With that he began. I admit that he took the first part of the concerto too fast, and the beginning consequently sounded helter-skelter; but later on, when I had a chance to indicate the tempo, he played as only he can play. It is significant that he played the cadenza, the most difficult part, best of all. His demeanour is worth any price to see. Not content with playing, he at the same time converses and makes comments, addressing a bright remark now to one, now to another of the assembled guests, nodding significantly to the right or left, particularly when something pleases him....

"In the adagio, and still more in the finale, he reached a climax, both as to his playing and the praise he had to bestow.

"A really divine episode I must not forget. Toward the end of the finale the second theme is, as you may remember, repeated in a mighty fortissimo. In the very last measures, when in the first triplets the first note is changed in the orchestra from G sharp to G, while the piano part, in a mighty scale passage, rushes wildly through the whole reach of the keyboard, he suddenly stopped, rose up to his full height, left the piano, and with big theatric strides and arms uplifted, walked across the large cloister hall, at the same time literally roaring the theme. When he got to the G in question he stretched out his arms imperiously and exclaimed: 'G, G, not G sharp! Splendid! That is the real Swedish Banko!' to which he added very softly, as in a parenthesis: 'Smetana sent me a sample the other day.' He went back to the piano, repeated the whole strophe, and finished. In conclusion, he handed me the manuscript, and said, in a peculiarly cordial tone: 'Keep steadily on; I tell you, you have the capability, and —do not let them intimidate you.'

"This final admonition was of tremendous importance to me; there was something in it that seemed to give it an air of sancti-fication. At times, when disappointment and bitterness are in store for me, I shall recall his words, and the remembrance of that hour will have a wonderful power to uphold me in days of adversity."

In performing Grieg's music, especially such works as the Concerto, the Ballade, Op. 24, and the "Slaater," Op. 72, we should constantly remember the heroic under-current of the composer's personality (so dramatically evinced by his brave behavior in Paris in connection with the Dreyfus affair) and the intensity of his emotionality. Sir Charles Villiers Stanford has called Grieg "a miniature viking," and there is much truth in this remark; for a certain fresh or tragic primitiveness, mixed with a somewhat eerie and ethereal spirituality, marks off Grieg's muse from that of Mid-European fellow-Romanticists such as Schumann or Chopin, and reveals more or less affinity with a similar "Northern" psychology in the works of other Norwegian creators in other branches of art, such as Ibsen, Björnson, Vinje, Arne Garborg, Munch, and Stefan Sinding.

Those that had the good fortune to hear Grieg perform his own compositions, whether as a pianist or as a conductor, are more likely to be alive to the heroic and intense attributes of his art than are those less lucky in this respect, for Grieg was nothing if not extremely virile and dynamic as an interpreter of his own works. Always a poet, but, above all, always a man. As a rule his *tempi* were faster than those usually heard in performances of Grieg works by other artists, and invariably the enthralling wistfulness and poetic appeal of his renderings knew no trace of sentimentality or mawkishness.

Strong and sudden accents of all kinds and vivid contrasts of light and shade were outstanding features of his self-interpretations, while the note of passion that he sounded was of a restless and feverish rather than of a violent nature. Extreme delicacy and exquisiteness of detail were present in his piano playing and altho the frailty of his physique, in his later years at least, withheld him from great displays of rugged force at the keyboard, he prized, and demanded, these resources in others, when occasion required.

In short, the general human tendencies of the heroic, active, poetic, excitably emotional Norwegian race from which he sprang all seemed to be faithfully portrayed in his renderings of his own compositions, as were, no less, the characteristics of the hillscapes and fjordscapes of his native land; for the brilliant coloring and striking clarity of the scenes, the almost indescribable exhilaration of the Northern atmosphere, all seem mirrored in his music.

Grieg eschewed all "muddiness" or turgid obscurity of tonal effect in writing for the piano or other instruments, and the performer of Grieg's music should

try to realise the composer's predilection for bright and clear and clean sonorities.

During the summer of 1907, while Grieg's guest at his country home "Troldhaugen," he and I spent much of our time rehearsing the concerto for a number of performances of the work to take place the following winter in the various capitals of Europe, himself conducting and myself playing the piano part. This tour was prevented by Grieg's death in September, 1907. But from our rehearsals of that summer I gleaned a, to me, priceless body of experiences anent Grieg's intentions regarding the rendering of the concerto, including expression marks written by Grieg himself into my score of the work as well as my notes descriptive of his own performances of the solo part. These data I have endeavored to place on record in the present publication. In this edition the original and authentic form of the concerto (i. e., as published in the latest edition sanctioned by Grieg himself) is represented by the music printed on the large staves marked I and II (with the exception of fingering and pedal marks, which are all mine thruout, and occasional alterations of the hand-divisions by me), while all alterations and suggestions emanating from my experiences with Grieg or otherwise offered by me and involving changes of notes, phrasing and dynamics, are shown in small notes on small staves *ABOVE* the piano solo part.

These alterations and suggestions fall into three classes:

(1) Those written by Grieg himself into my score of the concerto during the summer of 1907, or noted down by me as descriptive of his rendering during his performances of the work (marked E. G. in this edition).

(2) Those suggested to Grieg by me and approved of by him. These alterations (marked P. G. –E. G. in this edition) Grieg was planning to incorporate in future editions of the concerto.

(3) Those of a purely technical nature, not submitted to Grieg by me, but here offered to students as more effective or easier of execution than are the passages in question in their original forms (marked P. G. in this edition).

The "loud pedal" is indicated in this edition by the signs ⌐_____∧_∧_∫ ∪_∫, while the pressing down, holding and releasing of the "sostenuto" pedal is conveyed by the following signs: S. P...............✶

PERCY GRAINGER
New York City, May, 1919

29230

Concerto

FOR PIANO

(The orchestra arranged for a second piano)

Edited, revised, fingered, pedalled,
and with explanatory remarks,
by Percy Grainger

Edvard Grieg. Op. 16

*) The 32ds should be played *pp*, like delicate grace-notes.

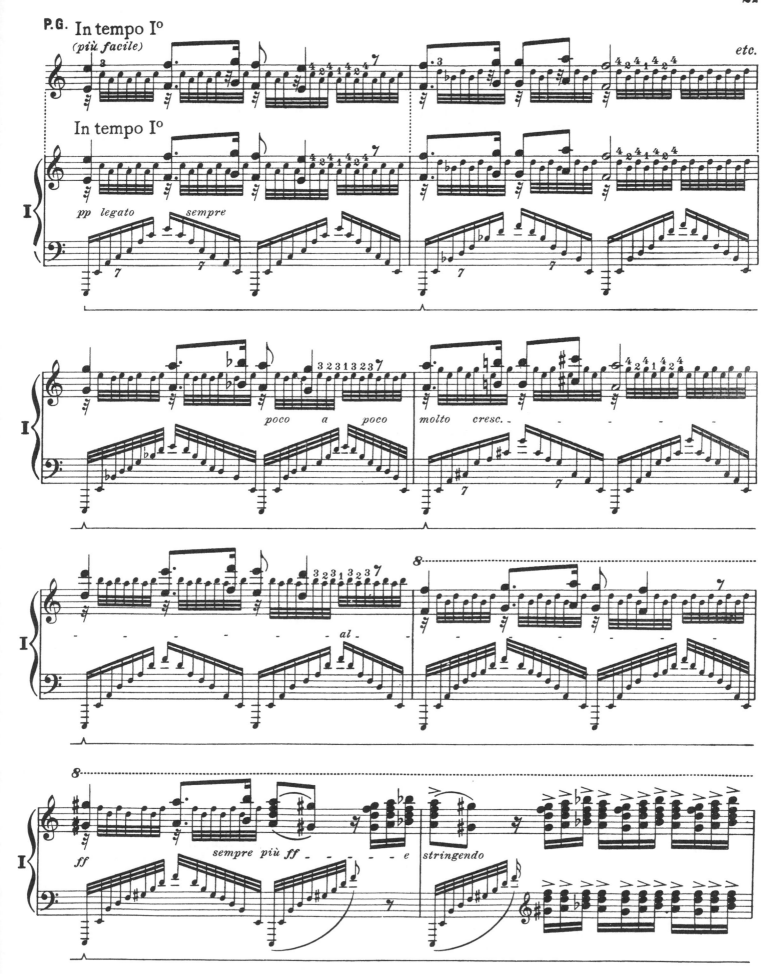

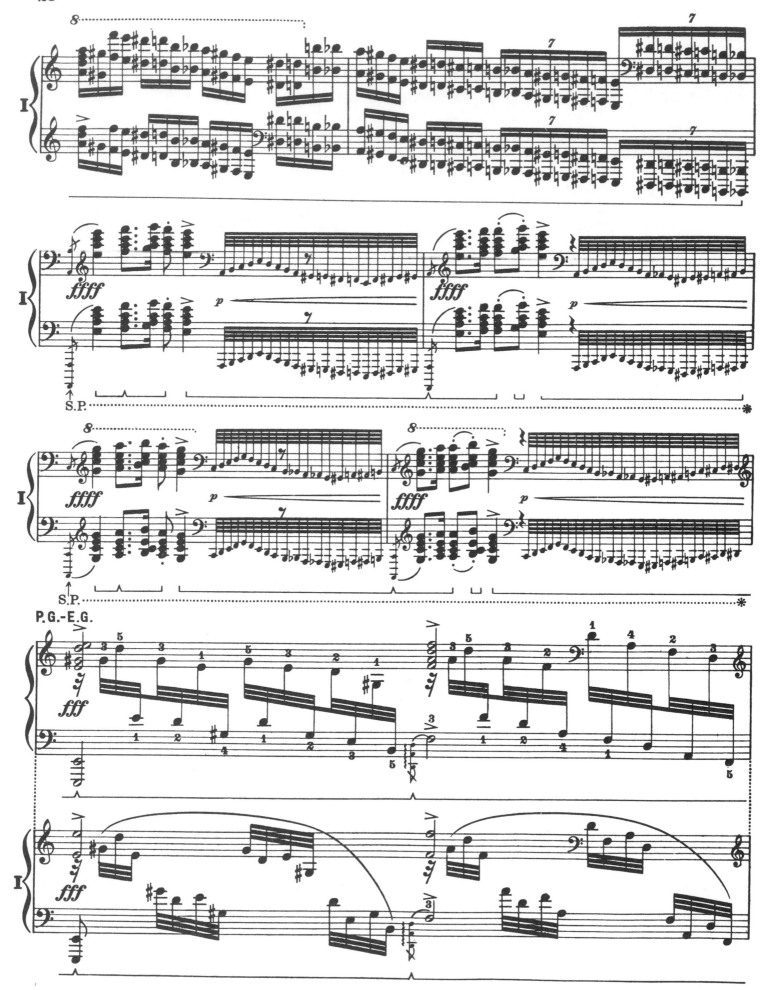

Grieg played the melody note E♭(at ✱) so loudly and the bass octave B♭♭(at ✱✱) so softly that at ✱✱ the former could clearly be heard singing on above the latter.

When playing with orchestra the pianist can execute the measure before the "poco animato" (which has a pause in Piano II) by regulating its duration as if it were two measures instead of one, duly advising the conductor in advance. By this means it is easier for the conductor to bring in the chord of the full orchestra exactly together with the last note of the pianist's run. The same applies to the runs in Piano I and the pauses in Piano II occuring one measure before A and one measure before F. The conductor should be advised in advance in all three cases.

Grieg wished the melodic basis of this passage, F#, F♮, E, to be very prominently heard.

The following rhythmic division of the passage-work was recommended to the editor by his teacher Professor James Kwast, as being advisable, in the interests of clarity and accuracy, owing to the rapid tempo of the movement.

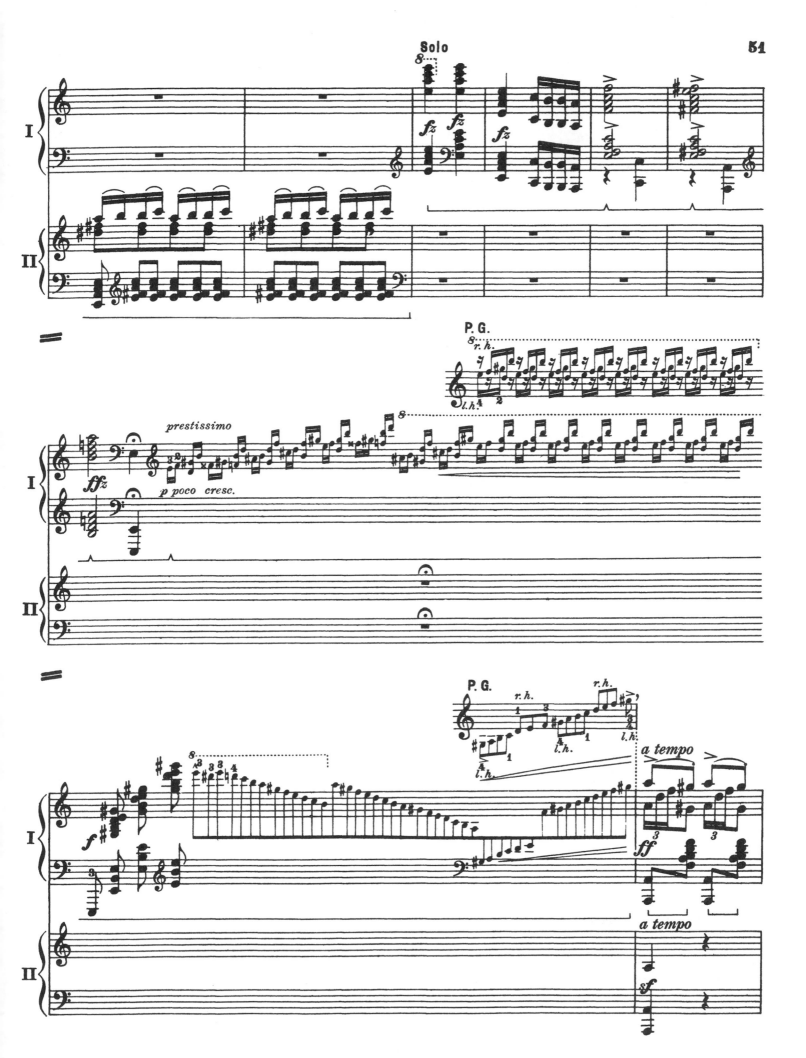

Poco piu tranquillo (♩ = 92)

Poco più tranquillo (♩ = 92)

Editor's note. Grieg played the following solo with restless, almost feverish emotionality, **but** without a trace of sentimentality. The louds and softs were very dramatically contrasted in his rendering of this section, and *tempo rubato* was freely used, without, however, the general speed being reduced from about M. M. ♩ = 92.

Recommended to the editor
by Professor James Kwast

P. G.
Andante maestoso
preceding
fff
I
Andante maestoso
preceding
ff
II
I
II